PRIVATE EYE

DUMB
BRITAIN 2

Published in Great Britain
by Private Eye Productions Ltd,
6 Carlisle Street, London W1D 3BN

www.private-eye.co.uk

© 2009 Pressdram Ltd
ISBN 987-1-901784-52-7
Designed by Bridget Tisdall
Printed in Great Britain by
Clays Ltd, St Ives plc

PRIVATE EYE

DUMB BRITAIN 2

Compiled by
MARCUS BERKMANN

Illustrated by Grizelda

**Real contestants, real quiz shows,
real answers, even more dumb!**

THE SYLLABUS

THE ABC

ANNE ROBINSON: What 'C' is a former German prisoner-of-war camp, which is now used as a scout hostel?

CONTESTANT: Auschwitz.

The Weakest Link

ANNE ROBINSON: Which 'P' is the smallest native British bat?

CONTESTANT: Pigeon.

The Weakest Link

ANNE ROBINSON: Which 'D' is a large city in the Republic of Ireland?

CONTESTANT: Belfast.

The Weakest Link

ANNE ROBINSON: What 'E' is the substance that forms a hard protective layer around the teeth?

CONTESTANT: Enema.

The Weakest Link

ANNE ROBINSON: What 'O' is a tea named after the Chinese word for dragon?

CONTESTANT: Ovaltine.

The Weakest Link

JOHNNY HERO: What 'R' is Hillary Clinton's maiden name?

MURIEL: Er, um, is it Rottweiler?

Downtown Radio, Northern Ireland

ANNE ROBINSON: Which 'S' is the only country to have a land border with Portugal?

PAGE 3 GIRL: Pass.

The Weakest Link

KAIT BORSAY: Give me two famous names beginning with S.

SECOND CONTESTANT: Simon Cowell.

BORSAY: And your second?

CONTESTANT: Er, pass. I can't think of one.

BORSAY: Just take a guess.

CONTESTANT: Erm, no, I can't think of one.

Quiz Call, five

ANNE ROBINSON: What 'V' is an adjective often used to describe the 7th-century Benedictine monk known as Bede?

CONTESTANT: Victor.

The Weakest Link

ANNE ROBINSON: In classical Greek drama what 'T' is the opposite of comedy?

CONTESTANT: Theatre.

The Weakest Link

KAIT BORSAY: Give me a famous name beginning with S.

CONTESTANT: Sir Alex Ferguson.

Quiz Call, five

ANNE ROBINSON: What 'Z' is a term used in literature to refer to a soft, gentle breeze?

CONTESTANT: Zippy.

The Weakest Link

ARCHITECTURE

JEREMY PAXMAN: Which famous structure, which opened in 1854, was designed by Isambard Kingdom Brunel?

STUDENT: The Eden Project.

University Challenge, BBC2

ART

ANNE ROBINSON: Which German painter was famous for his portraits of Henry VIII? Hans...

CONTESTANT: Solo.

The Weakest Link

PAUL BUNKER: Who painted the ceiling of the Sistine Chapel?

CALLER: Leonardo di Caprio.

2CR FM

BIOLOGY & NATURAL HISTORY

GARY KING: What is the largest carnivore that lives on the land?

CALLER: A whale.

LBC 97.3

ANNE ROBINSON: What type of bear lives in the Arctic?

CONTESTANT *(after much thought)*: Penguin.

The Weakest Link

GARY KING: What type of creature is a kingfisher?

CALLER: A fish?

LBC 97.3

JOHN HUMPHRYS: Which type of owl, with a distinctive white face, is named after the farm building where it nests?

YVETTE FIELDING: The snowy owl.

Celebrity Mastermind, BBC1

PRESENTER: Which of the following is not a deciduous tree: beech, cedar or oak?

CONTESTANT: Right. An evergreen tree is one that stays forever green. So deciduous is one that sheds its branches.

Are You Smarter Than A Ten-Year-Old?

STEVE WRIGHT: What was the animal referred to in Val Doonican's song 'Paddy McGinty's...'?

CALLER: I don't know.

WRIGHT: It begins with a 'G'.

CALLER: Cow.

BBC Radio 2

PRESENTER: Was the Tyrannosaurus Rex a carnivore or a herbivore?

CONTESTANT: No, it was a dinosore.

Are You Smarter Than A Ten-Year-Old?

JOHN HUMPHRYS: Which bird has species called grey, yellow and pied?

CONTESTANT: Piper.

Mastermind, BBC2

ANNE ROBINSON:
In nature, what
invertebrate has a
variable number of
limbs but a name
that literally means
'one hundred feet'?
CONTESTANT:
Giraffe.

The Weakest Link

ANNE ROBINSON: Cro-Magnon was an
early form of which mammal, which now
numbers in the billions?
CONTESTANT: Crabs.

The Weakest Link

ANNE ROBINSON: Which animal, bred for
meat, milk and wool, is unusual in that it is
spelt with two 'L's in its name?
CONTESTANT: The gnu.

The Weakest Link

ANNE ROBINSON: What type of cat is
renowned for never changing its spots?
CONTESTANT: Cheshire.

The Weakest Link

STEVE WRIGHT: What kind of creature is a
    kiwi?
CALLER: A fruit.

BBC Radio 2

SEAN STYLES: Trigger was the name of which
    famous cowboy's horse?
HELEN JONES: Long John Silver.

Presenters Mastermind, BBC Radio Merseyside

ANNE ROBINSON: The Cairngorms are
    home to Britain's last free-ranging herds of
    which animals, popularly associated with
    Christmas?
CONTESTANT *(pause)*: ...Turkeys?

The Weakest Link

CLASSICS &
ANCIENT HISTORY

ANNE ROBINSON: What was the principal language used by the ancient Romans?

CONTESTANT: Greek.

The Weakest Link

NOEL EDMUNDS: What is the last letter of the Greek alphabet?

CONTESTANT: Zulu.

Are You Smarter Than A Ten-Year-Old?

PAUL BUNKER: Who was the Roman god of war? I'll give you a clue. It's a type of chocolate bar.

CALLER: Twix.

2CR FM

ANNE ROBINSON: In mythology, what term for a potion that increases sexual desire is derived from the name of the Greek goddess of love?

WAG: Ooh! *(waves her arms about)* Ooh! I dead know it... Viagra!

The Weakest Link WAG Special

PRESENTER: What is the name of the lighthouse that was one of the Seven Wonders of the Ancient World?

CONTESTANT: Oh no! The only one I can think of is the needle thing – Cleopatra's Needle, which was one of the seven wonders of the world.

Are You Smarter Than A Ten-Year-Old?

PRESENTER: In Greek mythology, can you name one of the five rivers of Hades, the underworld?

CONTESTANT: Oh Gawd! I only know two rivers: the Thames and the Nile. It's got to be the Nile. Is it?

Are You Smarter Than A Ten-Year-Old?

CONTESTANT: I'd like to try Age 7 History please.

PRESENTER: What was the Roman name for the city of London?

CONTESTANT: I'm thinking. Do you know what I'm thinking? I think the Romans actually called it the same we did: they actually called it London.

Are You Smarter Than A Ten-Year-Old?

ANNE ROBINSON: In Roman numerals what letter represents a thousand?

CONTESTANT: Z.

The Weakest Link

JOHN HUMPHRYS: What letter is the Roman numeral for a thousand?

TOYAH WILCOX: V.

Celebrity Mastermind

ANNE ROBINSON: In which locality do the rivers Styx and Lethe flow, Hell or Halifax?

CONTESTANT *(after asking for question to be repeated and then thinking for a while)*: Halifax.

The Weakest Link

DOMESTIC SCIENCE

ANNE ROBINSON: Which savoury green fruit is often stuffed with pimento and served with cocktails?

CONTESTANT: Celery.

The Weakest Link

EAMONN HOLMES: Assam is what kind of beverage?

CONTESTANT (young male): Is it beer?

National Lottery Jet Set, BBC1

PRESENTER: Emmental and Double Gloucester are both types of what?

CALLER: Banks.

Breakfast Toaster Quiz, Heart FM

ANNE ROBINSON: Which hot drink is an anagram of the word 'eat'?

CONTESTANT: Hot chocolate.

The Weakest Link

ANNE ROBINSON: The food colouring E110 is also known as sunset what?

CONTESTANT: Boulevard.

The Weakest Link

PRESENTER: Right, I need this one, Sarah. Spinach is native to which continent?

SARAH: Er... er... er.... I think... well.... Sweden.

PRESENTER: That's a country. A wider continent.

SARAH: Oh I don't know.

PRESENTER: Have a guess, have a guess, any continent.

SARAH: Spain.

PRESENTER: That's another country.

SARAH (*laughs*): Oh is it?

PRESENTER: It starts with 'A'.

SARAH: Argentinia (*sic*).

PRESENTER: It's actually Asia, but never mind...

Fox FM

PRESENTER: What sweet has a name that sounds like a day of the week?

CALLER *(after long pause)*: Would it be marshmallow?

Radio Athlone

DRAMA

ANNE ROBINSON: Which musical starts with a cowboy singing 'Oh, What A Beautiful Morning'?

CONTESTANT: *Cabaret.*

The Weakest Link

ANNE ROBINSON: Opening in 2006, which West End musical features insulting Frenchmen, a limbless knight, and a killer rabbit?

CONTESTANT: *Chicago*.

The Weakest Link

ANNE ROBINSON: Which Stephen Sondheim musical's opening number includes the line 'He shaved the faces of gentlemen who never thereafter were heard of again'?

KRISTINA GRIMES: *Richard III*.

The Weakest Link:
'The Apprentice' special

ECONOMICS

ANNE ROBINSON: In the 1960s the then Chairman of British Rail proposed shutting down thousands of miles of railway lines. His name was Dr Richard what?

CONTESTANT: Branson.

The Weakest Link

ENGINEERING

ANNE ROBINSON: In which item of
household plumbing is it possible to
immerse the entire human body?

CONTESTANT: The u-bend.

The Weakest Link

ENGLISH LANGUAGE

ANNE ROBINSON: The English name for
each of the days of the week ends in what
letter?

CONTESTANT: D.

The Weakest Link

TERRY WOGAN: Which season is said to start on solstice day in December?

CONTESTANT 1: Spring?

WOGAN: In December, for God's sake?

CONTESTANT 2: Summer?

Wogan's Perfect Recall, C4

ANNE ROBINSON: When commuters are squashed together on trains, they are said to be packed in like what?

CONTESTANT: Eels.

The Weakest Link

ANNE ROBINSON: What word meaning deep and long-lasting sadness comes from two Greek words meaning 'black' and 'bile'?

CONTESTANT: Liquorice.

The Weakest Link

ANNE ROBINSON: The name of which card game is also the word for the upper bony part of the nose and a structure allowing a road to cross a river?

CONTESTANT: I don't know... Rummy.

The Weakest Link

ANNE ROBINSON:
    In education,
    what is a
    formal cap worn
    by academics,
    and also a piece
    of equipment
    used by
    bricklayers?
CONTESTANT:
    Trowel.
    The Weakest Link

ANNE ROBINSON: What surname was
    shared by a historical outlaw called
    'Butch' and a fictional cowboy called
    'Hopalong'?
CONTESTANT: Lesbian.

The Weakest Link

ANNE ROBINSON: In education, what
    name for a large lizard is also a term for a
    prefect?
CONTESTANT: Iguana.

The Weakest Link

ANNE ROBINSON: Which famous Englishman gave his name to both the water displacement level on a ship and a type of footwear worn in a gym?

CONTESTANT: Flip-flop.

The Weakest Link

ANNE ROBINSON: Simon, what means faithfulness in a relationship and is also a term used in sound reproduction?

ELIGIBLE BACHELOR *(after long pause)*: Dolby.

The Weakest Link: Eligible Bachelors Special

ANNE ROBINSON: RoSPA is the acronym for the Royal Society for the Prevention of what?

CONTESTANT: Animals.

The Weakest Link

ANNE ROBINSON: In the USA an unidentified dead body is sometimes known as a John what?

CONTESTANT: Wayne.

The Weakest Link

ANNE ROBINSON: Which direction of the compass is an anagram of the word 'shout'?

CONTESTANT: East.

The Weakest Link

ANNE ROBINSON: What three-letter word means 'at this moment'?

CONTESTANT: Then.

The Weakest Link

ANNE ROBINSON: If something in dispute is divided equally, it is referred to as splitting the... what?

CONTESTANT: Atom.

The Weakest Link

ENGLISH LITERATURE

STEVE YABSLEY: Which book by Graham Greene was set in Brighton?

CONTESTANT: *Fawlty Towers.*

BBC Radio Bristol

EAMONN HOLMES: What's the name of the playwright commonly known by the initials GBS?

CONTESTANT: William Shakespeare.

National Lottery Jet Set, BBC1

DERMOT MURNAGHAN: Complete the name of the Shakespeare play: *Troilus and....?*

CONTESTANT: Er... John.

Eggheads, BBC2

ANNE ROBINSON: Which Shakespeare play tells the story of an ill-fated love affair between a Roman general and an Egyptian queen?

CONTESTANT: The Merchant of Venice.

The Weakest Link

PRESENTER: Was Shakespeare born in Stoke-on-Trent, yes or no?

CALLER: Yes.

Century Radio

ANNE ROBINSON: In which H G Wells novel does an inventor travel in a machine of his own making?

CONTESTANT: The Simpsons.

The Weakest Link

ANNE ROBINSON: What 'B' was a pseudonym used by Charles Dickens?

CONTESTANT: Bart Simpson.

The Weakest Link

NE ROBINSON: Which famous writer fought in the Crimean War, Leo Tolstoy or Charles Dickens?

CONTESTANT: Charles Dickens.

The Weakest Link

ANNE ROBINSON: What was the name of the otter in the novel by Henry Williamson?

CONTESTANT: Dave.

The Weakest Link

ANNE ROBINSON: Who wrote *Far From The Madding Crowd*?

CONTESTANT: Timmy Mallett.

The Weakest Link

EAMONN HOLMES: Who wrote the novel *Tess Of The D'Urbervilles*?

CONTESTANT: Sherlock Holmes.

National Lottery Jet Set, BBC1

GEORGE BOWIE: What famous detective features in the Agatha Christie [sic] novel *The Hound of the Baskervilles*?

CONTESTANT: Is it Harry Potter?

Radio Clyde

ANNE ROBINSON: Audio tapes found in 2008 at the former home of the crime writer Agatha Christie revealed that her grandmother was the inspiration behind which of her fictional detectives?

CONTESTANT: Poirot.

The Weakest Link

WILLIAM G STEWART: Who wrote *The 39 Steps*?

CONTESTANT: Victor Silvester.

Fifteen-to-One, Challenge

PRESENTER: Where does Dracula come from?

CALLER *(after much thought)*: Pennsylvania.

Virgin Radio

STEVE WRIGHT:
Which legendary
bloodsucking
creature was
created by Bram
Stoker?

CALLER: The leech.

BBC Radio 2

ANNE ROBINSON: The novels by Dorothy
L Sayers feature the aristocratic detective
Lord Peter... who?

CONTESTANT: Snow.

The Weakest Link

ANNE ROBINSON: Which author wrote the
novels *Girls In Love*, *Girls Under Pressure*
and *Girls Out Late*?

CONTESTANT: Ernest Hemingway.

The Weakest Link

ANNE ROBINSON: Who wrote *Old Possum's
Book of Practical Cats*, which was made
into a musical by Andrew Lloyd Webber.

CONTESTANT: Er... Old Possum.

The Weakest Link

EAMONN HOLMES: Who wrote *The Catcher In The Rye*?

CONTESTANT: Chaucer.

National Lottery Jet Set, BBC1

STEVE WRIGHT: What was the name of the lioness depicted in Joy Adamson's book *Born Free*?

CALLER: Clarence.

BBC Radio 2

LISA SHAW: In which book is Room 101 a place to be feared?

CALLER: *101 Dalmatians*.

Century Radio Northeast

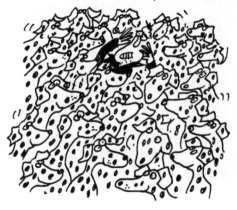

BRADLEY WALSH: What was the pen-name of the writer who based his bestselling books on his work as a vet in Yorkshire?

CONTESTANT: George Orwell.

Spin Star, ITV1

JOHN HUMPHRYS: Who was the actor who was knighted in 1953 and was a nephew of Ellen Terry?

CONTESTANT: George Orwell.

Mastermind, BBC2

ELLIOTT WEBB: Who wrote *Charlie And The Chocolate Factory*?

CALLER: Was it H G Wells?

96.4 BRMB, Birmingham

PRESENTER: Which French author has been translated into more languages than any other French author in the world?

CALLER: Chaucer.

LBC 97.3

ANNE ROBINSON: The British composer of The Sea Symphony and the opera The Pilgrim's Progress was Ralph Vaughan... what?

TAXI DRIVER NO. 467801: Chaucer.

The Weakest Link

JEREMY PAXMAN: Of all Beatrix Potter's books, which is the only one to feature a human in the title?

ANTONY BEEVOR, eminent author and historian: Peter Rabbit.

*University Challenge:
The Professionals, BBC2*

DARYL DENHAM: Which series of books by Enid Blyton featured a dog called Timmy?

CALLER: The Magnificent Five.

Virgin Radio

FASHION

EAMONN HOLMES: Where on the body would epaulets be worn?

CONTESTANT: On the legs.

National Lottery Jet Set, BBC1

FILM STUDIES

JON GAUNT: Which film is this quote taken from: 'You're gonna need a bigger boat'?

TRAFFIC REPORTER: Is it *Titanic*?

TalkSPORT

ANNE ROBINSON: In the James Bond films, the character played by Honor Blackman in *Goldfinger* was called Pussy what?

CONTESTANT: Finger.

The Weakest Link

GARY KING: Who sang the theme tune to the James Bond film *Goldfinger*?

CALLER: Shirley Temple.

LBC 97.3

STEVE WRIGHT: Who played agent 007 in the 1989 film *Licence To Kill*?

CALLER: James Bond, wasn't it?

BBC Radio 2

KIRSTY WARK: Winning in 1941 for the song 'The Last Time I Saw Paris', who was the first person called Oscar to win an Oscar?

CONTESTANT: Gene Kelly.

A Question of Genius, BBC2

ANNE ROBINSON: In film, the western starring John Wayne, James Stewart and Lee Marvin is called *The Man Who Shot Liberty*... who?

CONTESTANT: X.

The Weakest Link

ANNE ROBINSON: In which 1981 film did Dudley Moore star as the title character?

CONTESTANT: *10.*

The Weakest Link

DALE WINTON: Which fictional character was also called Lord Greystoke?

CONTESTANT: Lawrence of Arabia.

In It To Win It, BBC1

PRESENTER: Name a film beginning with the letter S.

CALLER: *Rocky.*

Quiz Call, five

RICHARD LEWIS: Which film released in 1984 starred Sigourney Weaver as a possessed cellist with a portal in her fridge?

CONTESTANT: Was it *I Am A Possessed Cellist With A Portal In My Fridge*?

BBC Radio Bristol

ANNE ROBINSON: Which actor played Quentin Crisp in the television film *The Naked Civil Servant*?

CONTESTANT: Mel Gibson.

The Weakest Link

ANNE ROBINSON: In the Carry On films, the actor who played characters named Pint Pot, Sir Roger de Lodgerly and Private Widdle was Charles who?

CONTESTANT: Windsor.

The Weakest Link

ANNE ROBINSON: The 1959 film by Alfred Hitchcock featuring two points of the compass in its name was called *North by North...* what?

CONTESTANT: South.

The Weakest Link

PRESENTER: Name a film with a person's name in the title.

CALLER: *Moby Dick*.

ANOTHER CALLER: *Black Beauty*.

YET ANOTHER CALLER: *Pearl Harbor*.

Quiz Call, five

STEVE WRIGHT: Johnny Weissmuller died on this day. Which jungle-swinging character clad only in a loincloth did he play?

CALLER: Jesus.

BBC Radio 2

GAMES

ANNE ROBINSON: Three stumps with two bails on top are essential equipment in which sport?

CONTESTANT: Horse racing.

The Weakest Link

ANNE ROBINSON: Which black American athlete won four gold medals at the 1936 Olympics?

CONTESTANT: Jesse James.

The Weakest Link

DERMOT MURNAGHAN: Where were the 1998 Commonwealth Games held?

CONTESTANT: Beijing.

Eggheads, BBC2

ANNE ROBINSON: In 1975 the first black tennis player to win the Wimbledon Men's Singles title was Arthur who?

CONTESTANT: Askey.

The Weakest Link

ANNE ROBINSON: Who won the US Open Tennis Championship wearing a black dress modelled on Audrey Hepburn's in *Breakfast at Tiffany's*?

CONTESTANT: Roger Federer.

The Weakest Link

JOHN MOODY: Which national football team have qualified eight times for the World Cup but have never progressed past the first round?

CONTESTANT: Celtic?

MOODY: No, national.

CONTESTANT: Oh, Arsenal.

Cash Cab, Challenge

ANNE ROBINSON: Which city was chosen to host the first Chinese Grand Prix in 2007?

CONTESTANT: Tokyo.

The Weakest Link

GARY KING: What did Babe Ruth play?

CALLER: Was it the trumpet, Gary?

LBC 97.3

RONNIE IRANI: In six nations rugby, what is the traditional emblem of the French team?

CONTESTANT: An onion?

TalkSPORT

ANNE ROBINSON: The point on a golf club or a tennis racket that gives the best contact is alliteratively known as the what spot?

CONTESTANT: The g-spot.

The Weakest Link

ANNE ROBINSON: What nickname is shared by a famous Scottish golfer and a British World War II general?

CONTESTANT: General Custer.

The Weakest Link

MIKE PARRY: Which team was runner-up to Lyon in the French First Division, taking the runner-up spot and entry into the Champions League?

CONTESTANT: Bordeaux?

PARRY: As in the Tapestry, yes?

CONTESTANT: Yes.

PARRY: That's the correct answer.

TalkSPORT

ANNE ROBINSON: In sporting folklore, the word 'golf' is often erroneously said to be an acronym of the phrase 'gentlemen only, ladies...' what?

CONTESTANT: Fornicate.

The Weakest Link

GEOGRAPHY

ANNE ROBINSON: Wainwright's Coast To Coast walk crosses three national parks. The North York Moors, the Yorkshire Dales and which other?

CONTESTANT: The Black Forest.

The Weakest Link

PRESENTER: Question one for ten pounds. The south of England is nearer the equator than the north of England. True or false?

CALLER: Ee that's a tricky one!

PRESENTER: The south of England is nearer the equator than the north of England. True or false?

CALLER: I'll go false.

Century FM

ALISON BELL: In which Devon resort was *Fawlty Towers* set?

CONTESTANT: Cornwall.

LBC 97.3

DARREN DAY: What area of Germany is the cake named after, that's made with chocolate, cream, kirsch and cherries?

CONTESTANT: Sorry if this isn't right, but is the answer Belgium?

Spin Star, ITV1

ANNE ROBINSON: In which European mountain range does the Matterhorn stand?

CONTESTANT: The Himalayas.

The Weakest Link

ANNE ROBINSON: 'Cornish' describes something as being from which English county?

CONTESTANT: Devon.

The Weakest Link

PRESENTER: What is the capital of Cuba?

CALLER: Ermmm.....

PRESENTER: Take your time.

CALLER: Ermmm...

PRESENTER: Go on, have a guess.

CALLER: Is it Belgium?

PRESENTER: Er, not quite.

Sun FM (Sunderland)

STEVE YABSLEY: What's the highest mountain in the UK?

CALLER: Mount Etna.

BBC Radio Bristol

PRESENTER: Mount Everest is in which mountain range?

CONTESTANT: It's in Nepal. So, I imagine, it would be the Andes.

Are You Smarter Than A Ten-Year-Old?

ANNE ROBINSON: What is the most northerly city in the British Isles?

CONTESTANT: Italy.

The Weakest Link

ANNE ROBINSON: Which Italian city is overlooked by Vesuvius?

CONTESTANT: Bombay.

The Weakest Link

ANNE ROBINSON: Which South American country has borders with ten others?

CONTESTANT: China.

The Weakest Link

JON GAUNT: Whereabouts in Italy are you from?

CALLER: I'll give you a clue – it's where they produce Parma ham...

GAUNT: Ah! Milano!

TalkSPORT

ANNE ROBINSON: Sri Lanka is situated to the south-east of which Asian country?

CONTESTANT: South Africa.

The Weakest Link

PRESENTER: What is the largest island in the Indian Ocean?

CALLER *(after lengthy consideration)*: Chile.

Lottery Quiz, Radio Devon

DALE WINTON: Alderney and Sark – are they part of the Channel Islands?

CONTESTANT: Ooooh! Is that the English Channel? I don't know, are there islands in the English Channel? I've never heard of any. France – that's near the English Channel isn't it?

In It To Win It, BBC1

DUMB COMPETITION

(From Flybe's in-flight menu, late 2007)

WIN A WEEKEND BREAK IN LONDON

Enter our competition and not only could you be off to London, we'll even treat you to a meal at Brian Turner's restaurant and a West End show.

HOW TO ENTER: For your chance to win, answer the following question:

What is the name of Flybe's celebrity chef?

Send your answer to Brian Turner Competition, c/o The Sandwich Factory Limited, Carlyon Road Industrial Estate...

ANNE ROBINSON: Pakistan was part
of which other state until it achieved
independence in 1947?

CONTESTANT: Bulgaria.

The Weakest Link

EAMONN HOLMES: What is the capital of
Cyprus?

CONTESTANT *(after much thought)*: Athens.

National Lottery Jet Set, BBC1

ANNE ROBINSON: A Catalan is an
inhabitant of a region in Spain known in
English as what?

CONTESTANT: Catatonia.

The Weakest Link

EAMONN HOLMES: Which British island
group are Tresco and St Mary's part of?

CONTESTANT: The West Indies.

National Lottery Jet Set, BBC1

JOHN LESLIE: If you spoke Dutch, what
country would you be from?

CALLER: Denmark.

This Morning, ITV

ANNE ROBINSON: In which continent is the river Danube?

PAGE 3 GIRL: France.

The Weakest Link

DAVE LEE TRAVIS: In which European country are there people called Walloons?

CALLER: Wales.

Breeze FM

ANNE ROBINSON: In which capital city will you find Gorky Park, Lenin's Tomb and St Basil's Cathedral?

CONTESTANT: London.

The Weakest Link

'MR ENGLAND' BEAUTY CONTEST
    PRESENTER: Which European city used to be called Constantinople?
MR BOURNEMOUTH: Er... is it Sweden?

My Crazy Life, C4

GRAHAM LIVER: In which country is Charles de Gaulle airport?
CONTESTANT: Russia.

BBC Radio Leeds

ANNE ROBINSON: Which 'U' is a South American country whose capital city is Montevideo?
CONTESTANT: Uganda.

The Weakest Link

ANNE ROBINSON: Which German city is also the name of a type of perfume?
CONTESTANT *(after much thought)*: Berlin.

The Weakest Link

ANNE ROBINSON: The National Assembly for Wales is based in which city?
CONTESTANT: Cork.

The Weakest Link

QUIZMASTER: Where is the Sea of
    Tranquillity?
CONTESTANT: Ibiza.

RI:SE, Channel 4

NICK FERRARI: Paris is bigger than Vienna.
    And Vienna is bigger than Rome. Which is
    the smallest?
FIRST CALLER: Vienna.
SECOND CALLER: Ooh, I dunno. Paris?

LBC 97.3

PAUL HARTLEY: Which ocean would you cross if you sailed from San Francisco to Sydney? This is the world's largest ocean.

CALLER: The Mediterranean.

BBC Radio Humberside

PRESENTER: What canal connects the Atlantic Ocean to the Pacific Ocean?

CALLER: Er... um...

PRESENTER: It has the same name as a type of cigar...

CALLER: Is it the Hamlet canal?

BBC Radio Nottingham

MATHEMATICS

ANNE ROBINSON: In maths, what is one half as a decimal?

CONTESTANT: A quarter.

The Weakest Link

ANNE ROBINSON: What imperial measurement is made up of 12 inches?

CONTESTANT: A centimetre, Anne.

The Weakest Link

MIKE PARRY: How many leaves are there on a four-leaf clover?

CONTESTANT: Three.

TalkSPORT

KEN BRUCE: Name that group. There are three of them in it.

CONTESTANT: Was it the Four Tops?

BBC Radio 2

TERRY WOGAN: In The Sound Of Music, what age was Liesl going to be next birthday? She was sixteen going on...

CONTESTANT: Five.

Wogan's Perfect Recall, Channel 4

PRESENTER: Bob Hope was the fifth of how many sons?

CALLER: Four.

LBC 97.3

ANNE ROBINSON: What kind of dozen is 13?

CONTESTANT: Half a dozen.

The Weakest Link

CONTESTANT: I think I'll try 'Age 6 Maths'.

PRESENTER: Add the number of Goldilocks' bears to the maids a-milking your true love sent.

CONTESTANT: There were three bears... and I think there were eight maids. Let me see, three and eight is eleven... er... I think. I'll check. Can I borrow your fingers?

Are You Smarter Than A Ten-Year-Old?

MIKE PARRY: How many Christmases took place during the Second World War?

CONTESTANT: Fifty-eight.

TalkSPORT

54

ANNE ROBINSON: What is the highest prime number under ten?

OXFORD RESEARCH FELLOW: Eleven.

The Weakest Link

MIKE PARRY: How many 'r's are there in 'irreversible'?

CALLER: Twelve.

TalkSPORT

CONTESTANT: I'd like to try Age 6 Maths, Noel.

NOEL EDMONDS: How many days will there be in the year 2010?

CONTESTANT: Er... is it 60 or 52?

Are You Smarter Than A Ten-Year-Old?

MALE PRESENTER: Guess how many hours sleep you lose in a year looking after a new born baby.

FEMALE PRESENTER: What, in all 352 days?

MALE PRESENTER (*laughs loudly*): Don't you mean 356?

FEMALE PRESENTER: OK, in a leap year, right.

Real Radio

PRESENTER: If I travel at 60 miles an hour, how far do I travel in ten minutes?

CALLER: Two hundred thousand miles.

GMTV

JAMIE THEAKSTON: How many days are left from today until the end of this year?

CONTESTANT: How long do I have to work it out?

THEAKSTON: Five more seconds.

CONTESTANT: Er... 700?

Heart FM

IAIN LEE: How many people in Islington at the last census put their profession down as 'Finance'?

CALLER: One million.

Virgin Radio

MEDIA STUDIES

MIKE PARRY: You read the papers. How was Britain involved in tit-for-tat diplomacy this week?

CALLER: The Sun? Page 3?

TalkSPORT

ANNE ROBINSON: Which first name is shared by a singer with the surname O'Connor and an actress with the surname Cusack?

CONTESTANT: Des.

The Weakest Link

ANNE ROBINSON: The television presenter and forecaster who was head of the BBC Weather Centre from 1991 to 2000 was Bill who?

CONTESTANT: Gates.

The Weakest Link

DUMB BLUE

DUNCAN JAMES of the boyband Blue: I'm thinking, age 7 English grammar. What's grammar?

NOEL EDMONDS: If you need to ask you might be better with something else.

DUNCAN JAMES (to young Joseph): How old are you?

(Joseph is too stunned to reply)

NOEL EDMONDS: Ten.

DUNCAN JAMES: Yeah, obviously.

NOEL EDMONDS: There's a clue in the title of the show.

NOEL EDMONDS: Age 9 world geography. Cheryl is in Ethiopia, Kimberley is in Kenya and Sarah is in Sudan. Which girl's in a landlocked country?

DUNCAN JAMES: What does 'a landlocked country' mean?

NOEL EDMONDS: I had a feeling you were going to ask that.

Celebrity Are You Smarter Than A Ten-Year-Old, Sky One

ANNE ROBINSON: Who is one of the team
   captains of *Have I Got News For You* and
   is also the editor of Private Eye?

CONTESTANT: Gary Lineker.

The Weakest Link

MO DUTTA: What is the surname of the actor
   Peter who plays Cleggy in *Last Of The
   Summer Wine*?

CALLER: Sorry, I don't know.

DUTTA: He's famous and he's been in the
   show for years.

CALLER: Sorry, I don't know.

DUTTA: It was Sallis.

CALLER: I didn't know Peter Sellers was in
   Last Of The Summer Wine.

BBC Radio 2

LES DENNIS: Other than Family Fortunes, name a TV show with the word 'family' in the title.

CONTESTANT: *The Generation Game*.

SECOND CONTESTANT (same family): *The Brady Bunch*.

Family Fortunes, Challenge

RICHARD LEWIS: Who wrote and performed the poem 'Oh I wish I'd looked after my teeth'?

CONTESTANT: I don't know this...

LEWIS: OK, shall I do the voice?

CONTESTANT: Go for it.

LEWIS: Who wrote and performed the poem [puts on west country accent] 'Oh I wish I'd looked after me teeth?'

CONTESTANT: I'll go for Benny Hill.

BBC Radio Bristol

ANNE ROBINSON: Peter Brough, the 1950s radio ventriloquist, had a dummy whose name was Archie... what?

CONTESTANT: Gemmill.

The Weakest Link

RAY HOUGHTON: Name the famous comedian who claims to come from Kazakhstan.

CONTESTANT: Russ Abbot.

TalkSPORT

TERRY WOGAN: Which Duke resides at Woburn Abbey?

CONTESTANT: Hazzard.

Wogan's Perfect Recall, Channel 4

MEDICINE

ANNE ROBINSON: The 17th-century physician who discovered the true nature of the circulation of blood around the human body was William who?

CONTESTANT: Shatner.

The Weakest Link

ANNE ROBINSON: What 'G' is the area of medicine specialising in the treatment of the elderly?

CONTESTANT: Gynaecology.

The Weakest Link

STEVE WRIGHT: On what part of the body is a lobotomy performed?

CONTESTANT: The bottom.

BBC Radio 2

ANNE ROBINSON: Gynaecology is concerned with the health of which sex?

FEMALE CONTESTANT: Men.

The Weakest Link

ANNE ROBINSON: A cochlea implant is designed to stimulate which of the five senses?

CONTESTANT: Could you repeat that please, Anne?

The Weakest Link

MILITARY HISTORY

ANNE ROBINSON: Which of the three
British armed forces is known as 'the senior
service'?

CONTESTANT (and eventual winner): The SS.

The Weakest Link

LES ROSS: In the British army, which rank is
next highest after Captain?

CALLER: Admiral.

BBC Radio WM

PRESENTER: Which ancient army was
discovered in China in 1974?

CONTESTANT: The Territorial Army.

Metro Radio

MODERN HISTORY

NEMONE: In which battle was Lord Horatio
Nelson fatally wounded?

CALLER: The Battle of Hastings.

BBC 6 Music

PRESENTER: What was the date of the Battle of Hastings?

CONTESTANT: Ooooh! Er.... was it 1974?

Galaxy Radio, Leeds

FRED MACAULEY: What date was the Great Fire of London?

CALLER: 1066.

BBC Radio Scotland

PRESENTER: Here's question two, for 20 pounds. The Great Fire of London occurred in 1966. True or false?

CALLER: I'll go true.

Century FM

PRESENTER: What official title was given to
    Thomas Becket in 1162?

CONTESTANT: I was going to say 'Sir'. I
    know he was important. I think it's 'Sir
    Thomas Becket.'

Are You Smarter Than A Ten-Year-Old?

ANNE ROBINSON: The medieval map of
    the world housed in Hereford Cathedral is
    known as the Mappa what?

CONTESTANT: The world.

The Weakest Link

ANNE ROBINSON: Leonardo da Vinci,
    Martin Luther and Christopher Columbus
    were all born in which century?

CONTESTANT *(after long pause)*: The
    twentieth.

The Weakest Link

ANNE ROBINSON: In 1613 a misfiring
    cannon caused a fire that burned down
    which theatre during a performance of
    Shakespeare's Henry VIII?

CONTESTANT: Crystal Palace.

The Weakest Link

ANNE ROBINSON: How many of his wives did Henry VIII divorce?

ELIGIBLE BACHELOR: Eight.

The Weakest Link: Eligible Bachelors Special

GARY PHILLIPSON: What was the profession of Louis VIII?

CALLER: Er, I don't know. Was he a doctor?

TFM 96.6, Cleveland

JOHN HUMPHRYS: When the Ashmolean opened in Beaumont Street in Oxford in 1683, it was the first public what?

BILL KENWRIGHT: Convenience.

Celebrity Mastermind, BBC1

ANNE ROBINSON: In the English monarchy, what was the name of the Royal house that succeeded the Tudors?

CONTESTANT: Buckingham Palace.

The Weakest Link

ANNE ROBINSON: Nelson's flagship HMS Victory was constructed mainly of which wood?

CONTESTANT: Balsa.

The Weakest Link

ANNE ROBINSON: In 1812, Napoleon Bonaparte lost over half his army in the disastrous invasion of which eastern European empire?

CONTESTANT: France.

The Weakest Link

ALAN BRAZIL: Which country hasn't fought a war since 1815?

RONNIE IRANI: I'll give you a clue. It's a famously neutral country co-hosting Euro 2008.

CALLER: Is it Austria?

TalkSPORT

PAUL BUNKER: Question two. What year did the Titanic sink?

CALLER: Oh blimey. It's got to be 1940-something. 45? Something like that?

CAROLINE VERDON: The year that the war started.

PAUL: No, the war ended in '45, Caroline.

CAROLINE: My history is so bad.

2CR FM

ANNE ROBINSON: Which English queen rode a chariot with knives on the wheels?

CONTESTANT *(full of confidence)*: Victoria!

The Weakest Link

PRESENTER: Queen Victoria's husband, Albert, was a relative of hers before they were married. How were they related?

CONTESTANT: I don't think he was her father. I think they were both the same age. I wonder if they were brother and sister?

Are You Smarter Than A Ten-Year-Old?

ANNE ROBINSON: What is the name of the nurse who rose to fame in the Crimean War and was named after the Italian city where she was born?

CONTESTANT: Frances Nightingale.

The Weakest Link

ANNE ROBINSON: On June 7th each year, Norway celebrates its 1905 independence from which other European country?

CONTESTANT: Canada.

The Weakest Link

ANNE ROBINSON: Who was the Norwegian explorer who first reached the South Pole?

CONTESTANT: Sherpa Tenzing.

The Weakest Link

ANNE ROBINSON: Which Joseph founded a famous chain of teashops, the first one opening in London in 1894?

HUGO *(confidently)*: Goebbels.

The Weakest Link

ANNE ROBINSON: During World War II, in June 1940, Paris was captured by troops from the army of which country?

CONTESTANT: England.

The Weakest Link

ANDY COLLINS: Name a famous historical heroine.

CONTESTANT: Winston Churchill.

Family Fortunes, ITV

BILLY BUTLER: What was Hitler's first name?

CONTESTANT: Heil.

BBC Radio Merseyside

ANNE ROBINSON: What 'T' did British POWs use to escape from Second World War German prison camps?

CONTESTANT: I don't know. Was it herbal?

The Weakest Link

MODERN LANGUAGES

ANNE ROBINSON: In seafood on a restaurant menu, the French word 'poisson' literally translates into English as what?

CONTESTANT: Chicken.

The Weakest Link

CONTESTANT: I'll try Age 7 French, please.

NOEL EDMONDS: What is the English translation of the French word 'voiture'?

CONTESTANT: It's not a colour, not a number. It could sound similar.

EDMONDS: Similar to what?

CONTESTANT: An English word. A tree.

Are You Smarter Than A Ten-Year-Old?

MUSIC

DERMOT MURNAGHAN: The name of which percussion instrument literally means 'wood sound' in Greek?

CONTESTANT: Sorry, I haven't got a clue.

MURNAGHAN: Go on, have a guess. Percussion instrument.

CONTESTANT: Flute?

Eggheads, BBC2

STEVE WRIGHT: The leader of the orchestra plays which musical instrument?

CALLER: The baton.

BBC Radio 2

EAMONN HOLMES: What does J S Bach's middle initial stand for?

CONTESTANT: Stewart.

National Lottery Jet Set, BBC1

CHRIS MOYLES: Florence, from Florence and the Machine, is named after which Italian city?

CALLER: Rome.

BBC Radio 1

ULRIKA JONSSON: Which composer wrote the collection of musical works known as The Planets?

CONTESTANT: Tolstoy.

Dog Eat Dog, BBC1

ANNE ROBINSON: The famous operatic aria Nessun Dorma can be translated as 'None Shall...' what?

CONTESTANT: Walk.

The Weakest Link

GARY KING: Name the music festival started in 1895 by Sir Henry Wood.

CALLER: Glastonbury.

LBC 97.3 FM

CHRIS BROOKS: What year was the term 'disc jockey' first used?

CONTESTANT: 1720.

Capital Radio

ANNE ROBINSON: The story by Herman Melville that was made into an opera by Benjamin Britten was called Billy... what?

CONTESTANT: Bunter.

The Weakest Link

JOHN HUMPHRYS: Who had their first hit in the British singles chart in 1963 with 'Surfin' USA'?

CONTESTANT: Er, the Sex Pistols.

Mastermind, BBC2

RICHARD LEWIS: EMI sacked which band after their appearance on the Today show.

CONTESTANT: Oh erm... was he the one that was in Celebrity Get Me Out Of Here?

LEWIS: Ooh, close!

CONTESTANT: I'm gonna go for the Bay City Rollers.

BBC Radio Bristol

ANNE ROBINSON: What surname is shared by a jazz pianist called Scott and a rock singer called Janis?

CONTESTANT: Street-Porter.

The Weakest Link

ANNE ROBINSON: What was the surname of Rex and Noel, who had hits respectively with 'If I Could Talk To The Animals' in 1967 and 'Windmills Of Your Mind' in 1968?

CONTESTANT: Kissinger.

The Weakest Link

MIKE PARRY: What name does Cat Stevens go under now? I'll give you a clue, he converted to Isl... er, he became a Muslim...

CALLER: Abu Hamza?

TalkSPORT

ANNE ROBINSON: Which pop group, who once collaborated on a record with the footballer Paul Gascoigne, took their name from an island off the coast of Northumberland?

CONTESTANT: Gerry and the Pacemakers.

The Weakest Link

NICK PANDOLFI: Which Liverpool club became famous as the venue for many of the Beatles' early gigs?

CALLER: Everton.

BBC Radio Suffolk

ALAN BRAZIL: Which Beatles album was the last one they recorded?

RONNIE IRANI: Here's your clue. It has a very famous picture on the cover.

CALLER: Mona Lisa.

BRAZIL: Difficult questions this morning, Ronnie.

TalkSPORT

ANNE ROBINSON: In 2007, former Rolling Stone Bill Wyman launched his signature brand of which portable device used by treasure hunters?

CONTESTANT: Mine detector.

The Weakest Link

JAMES O'BRIEN: Which song was made famous by the animated Raymond Briggs film, The Snowman?

CALLER: 'Singing In The Rain'.

LBC 97.3

RICHARD LEWIS: Complete the lyrics of this hit song by northern singer Lisa Stansfield: 'I may not be a lady but I'm...'?

CONTESTANT: Er... not a man?

BBC Radio Bristol

MIKE PARRY: Which two singers are teaming up to sing the theme tune for the new James Bond film, *Quantum of Solace*?

CALLER: Is it Elvis Presley and Roy Orbison?

TalkSPORT

ANNE ROBINSON: In a concert at the London Astoria in 1967, who set his guitar on fire for the very first time?

CONTESTANT: Neil Diamond.

The Weakest Link

NICK FERRARI: What was the title of the Beatles' fifth album?

CALLER: I don't know.

FERRARI: A four-letter word beginning with H.

CALLER: A Hard Day's Night.

LBC 97.3

MARK GOODIER: Can you name David Bowie's wife?

CALLER: Is it Imran Khan?

Smooth Radio

MYTH & LEGEND

ANNE ROBINSON: In legend, Uther Pendragon was the father of which king?

CONTESTANT: Charles.

The Weakest Link

MARK CHAPMAN: Who did William Tell supposedly shoot an apple off the head of?

LAURA (assistant producer): Was it a king?

CHAPMAN: No, it wasn't.

LAURA: Was it Robin Hood?

CHAPMAN: No.

LAURA: Einstein?

CHAPMAN: No.

LAURA: He had something to do with apples, didn't he?

BBC Radio 1

PRESENTER: According to legend, who shot an apple off the top of his son's head?

CONTESTANT: Well, straightaway I'm thinking of Isaac Newton.

Are You Smarter Than A Ten-Year-Old?

POLITICS

ANNE ROBINSON: In UK politics, who was the only former leader of the Labour Party to become a European Commissioner?

CONTESTANT: Margaret Thatcher.

The Weakest Link

ROBERT ROBINSON: Which British Prime Minister was born in Yorkshire in 1852?

CONTESTANT: Jim Callaghan.

Brain Of Britain, Radio 4

ANNE ROBINSON: Archie Stirling, who launched the Scottish Voice Party in 2007, is the nephew of Sir David Stirling, who in 1941 founded which elite fighting force?

CONTESTANT: The Liberal Democrats.

The Weakest Link

JOHN HUMPHRYS: Who is the daughter of Vera Brittain who was one of the co-founders of the Social Democratic Party?

CONTESTANT: David Owen.

Mastermind, BBC2

JAMES PEIKOS: Who was the leader of the Labour Party before Tony Blair?

CALLER: John Major.

Viking FM

PRESENTER: Who was the Prime Minister before Tony Blair?

CALLER: George Bush.

Century FM

ANNE ROBINSON: In 1948 David Ben-Gurion became Prime Minister of which country?

CONTESTANT: Wales.

The Weakest Link

OWEN MONEY: In 30 seconds, name as many well-known politicians as you can.

CALLER: Er, Tony Brown. And Nigel Benn. *(Silence.)*

BBC Radio Wales

ANNE ROBINSON: The Irish President, elected in 1990, who was the first to visit a British monarch, was Mary who?

CONTESTANT: Mary Queen of Scots.

The Weakest Link

PRESENTER: Which Boris recently became Mayor of London?

MIKEY (from *Big Brother*): Yeltsin.

PRESENTER: No, it was Boris Johnson. Which publication was Boris Johnson the editor of?

MIKEY: The Sun.

BBC Radio Scotland

ANNE ROBINSON: The name of the Minister of Transport who gave his name to a type of pedestrian crossing was Leslie Hore-... what?

CONTESTANT: Pelican.

The Weakest Link

ANNE ROBINSON: At the Conservative Party conference in 2002, which politician said, 'Do not underestimate the determination of a quiet man'?

CONTESTANT: Neil Kinnock.

The Weakest Link

MIKE PARRY: Which high-profile South American President and outspoken critic of the US recently visited Iran?

CONTESTANT: Ennio Morricone.

TalkSPORT

ANNE ROBINSON: Which actress sang 'Happy Birthday to you' to John F Kennedy?

CONTESTANT: The Queen.

The Weakest Link

ANNE ROBINSON: In Russian politics, Vladimir Putin is renowned as an accomplished performer of which activity, Judo or Cluedo?

CONTESTANT: Cluedo.

The Weakest Link

RACHEL (producer): Name Prince Charles's younger sister.

CALLER: Is it Camelia?

The Ugly Phil Breakfast Show, Kerrang! Radio

DUMB LAMMY

(Answers given by David Lammy MP on an edition of Celebrity Mastermind, BBC1, December 28th 2008)

JOHN HUMPHRYS: What was the married name of the scientists Marie and Pierre, who won the Nobel Prize for Physics in 1903 for their research into radiation?

DAVID LAMMY: Antoinette.

HUMPHRYS: Which fortress was built in the 1370s to defend one of the gates of Paris and was later used as a state prison by Cardinal Richelieu?

LAMMY: Versailles.

HUMPHRYS: Which variety of blue English cheese traditionally accompanies port?

LAMMY: Leicester.

HUMPHRYS: Who acceded to the English throne at the age of 9 on the death of his father Henry VIII in 1547?

LAMMY: Henry VII.

RELIGIOUS STUDIES

ANNE ROBINSON: What is the Christian name of the Archbishop of Canterbury? It's also the name of a native British tree?

CONTESTANT: Yew.

The Weakest Link

ANNE ROBINSON: The garden at Gethsemane in Jerusalem is at the foot of the Mount of... what?

CONTESTANT: Everest.

The Weakest Link

PRESENTER: Who in the Christian Bible was thrown into a den of lions: Samuel, Nathaniel or Daniel?

CONTESTANT (student teacher): The first thing that came into my head was Samuel. It's not Nathaniel, I'm sure. Eeny meeny miny mo.

PRESENTER: You've stopped at Daniel.

CONTESTANT: Yes, but I'm going with Samuel.

Are You Smarter Than A Ten-Year-Old?

PRESENTER: On what day do Christians celebrate Jesus being nailed to the cross?

CONTESTANT: I think it's Good Friday or the Bank Holiday weekend, which ends on Sunday.

Are You Smarter Than A Ten-Year-Old?

PRESENTER: According to the Old Testament, on which mountain did Moses receive the Ten Commandments?

CONTESTANT: Ah, I think I know this one. Something tells me it's Mount Rushmore.

Are You Smarter Than A Ten-Year-Old?

ANNE ROBINSON: In the Bible, which city, along with Gomorrah, was destroyed by God because of its wickedness?

CONTESTANT: Nazareth.

The Weakest Link

ANNE ROBINSON: Castel Gandolfo is the summer residence of which religious leader?

CONTESTANT: Jesus.

The Weakest Link

PRESENTER: What religion was Guy Fawkes?

CALLER: Jewish.

PRESENTER: That's close enough.

BRMB

PRESENTER: Along with two fishes, how many loaves of bread did Jesus use to feed the five thousand?

CONTESTANT: When this question first came up, I thought four, but now I think it may have been six. It could have been eight, but now fourteen seems to ring a bell.

Are You Smarter Than A Ten-Year-Old?

ANNE ROBINSON: In the New Testament the gospels are attributed to Mark, Luke, John and who else?

CONTESTANT: Jesus.

The Weakest Link

ANNE ROBINSON: In the Bible, which man, who lived to 969 years old, was the grandfather of Noah?

CONTESTANT: God.

The Weakest Link

ANNE ROBINSON: In Roman Catholicism, baptism, confirmation and matrimony are three of the seven what?

CONTESTANT: Deadly sins.

The Weakest Link

SCIENCE & TECHNOLOGY

ANNE ROBINSON: What man-made structure built during the 3rd century BC is often said to be visible from space?

CONTESTANT: The Millennium Dome.

The Weakest Link

JOHN HUMPHRYS: In September 1783, a sheep, a rooster and a duck were the first passengers ever to travel on which form of transport?

CONTESTANT: A hovercraft.

Mastermind, BBC2

JEREMY PAXMAN: Regarded as a co-operating state since 1979, which is the only non-European country to participate in the European space agency?

SHEFFIELD STUDENT: Turkey.

PAXMAN: No. Anyone want to buzz from Murray Edwards College?

MURRAY EDWARDS STUDENT: Turkey.

University Challenge, BBC2

LES ROSS: Which form of London public transport was pioneered by George Shillibeer in 1829?

CALLER: The M25.

BBC Radio WM

STEVE POWERS: What does a planet orbit around?

CALLER 1: The galaxy?

CALLER 2: The moon?

Wave 105FM

DANNY KELLY: Which prominent Birmingham family had a toposcope constructed in 1923 for the top of Beacon Hill in the Lickey Hills?

CALLER: The Osbournes.

BBC Radio WM

CHRIS TARRANT: Which country launched the Skylab space station in 1973?

ALASTAIR CAMPBELL: France is my final answer.

Celebrity Who Wants To Be A Millionaire?, ITV

DARWIN'S THEORY OF COMPUTER EVOLUTION

ANNE ROBINSON: Charles who is said to be the father of modern electronic computing?
CONTESTANT: Darwin.

The Weakest Link

DJ: Which piece of modern technology is named after King Harald I of Denmark, who lived between 910 and 985 AD?
CALLER: Photocopier.

Magic FM

MULTIPLE CHOICE

ANNE ROBINSON: What is a singlet: a bachelor or a vest?
ELIGIBLE BACHELOR: A bachelor.

The Weakest Link: Eligible Bachelor Special

ANNE ROBINSON: What is a
     divertimento: an Italian road sign or a piece
     of music?
FASHION PERSON: An Italian road sign.

The Weakest Link: Fashion Special

ANNE ROBINSON: According to legend, a
     causeway was built between Ireland and
     Scotland for whom to cross: giants or
     leprechauns?
CONTESTANT: Leprechauns.

The Weakest Link

PRESENTER: Edinburgh Zoo has opened a
     new enclosure called the Budongo trail.
     What kind of animals are housed there,
     chimpanzees or budongos?
CALLER: Budongos.

Real Radio

ANNE ROBINSON: In olden times, what
     were minstrels: travelling entertainers or
     chocolate salesmen?
CONTESTANT: Chocolate salesmen.

The Weakest Link

R.I.P.

ANNE ROBINSON: In maths, if the number 10 is doubled, what is the result?

JADE GOODY: 30.

The Weakest Link